The Child's Geography - Primary Source Edition

Mark James Barrington- Ward

PART I.

FIRST LESSONS IN GEOGRAPHY.

CONTENTS.

I HAVE been for some time convinced that the manuals of rudimentary geography now used in English schools are, for the most part, constructed on wrong principles. In teaching, and in examining, I have again and again seen how difficult it is for a child to acquire geographical information by means of mere memory lessons. Set formulæ are learnt by heart, long strings of names are committed to memory, simple explanation of new terms is ignored, the map is but little used, and the child's own observing powers are not cultivated. Hence it comes that geography is at first an unpalatable subject to a child, and the amount of benefit which he derives from it is very limited.

With a view to supply, in some little measure, the acknowledged want of a rudimentary geography which shall teach the first facts and principles simply, and yet thoroughly, I have compiled the following pages. Should the book meet with a favourable reception, it will be followed by two others of wider scope, elementary and advanced.

I write for children, be it remembered, and I use at first only the limited set of words found in the ordinary vocabulary of a child seven or eight years of age. By degrees harder words are introduced, with explanations. A very ample set of questions and hints for young teachers will be found at the bottom of each page. The separate lessons are very short, but, in revision, it will often be found desirable to take two or three of them together. Reliance has been placed upon ample pictorial illustration.

M. J. B. W.

St. Winifred's, Lincoln.

MOUNTAINS, HILLS, VALLEY, TABLE-LAND, RIVER, BRIDGE.

THE CHILD'S GEOGRAPHY.—FIRST LESSONS.

LESSON I.*

1. About Geography.—We have now to begin a study called GEOGRAPHY. It will tell us a great deal about the Earth—that is, the World on which we live. We shall hear much that is pleasant and useful to know, and we shall not find it at all hard to learn, if we only pay a little attention.

The word Geography means a description of the Earth.

2. This Earth of which I have just spoken is an immense ball or globe. On its surface, or outside, we live, and there, too, we find all kinds of plants and animals. The surface of the World is made up of land and water only.

3. About Land and Water.—You all know the difference between land and water, I suppose, and I need hardly tell you how different a river is from its banks, or the sea from its shores. Most of us usually spend our time on the land, but we are able to move about on the waters, even when they are very broad, by means of boats and ships. Some people, called sailors, pass nearly all their days going in this way from one place to another.

QUESTIONS AND SUGGESTIONS FOR THE USE OF THE TEACHER.
The suggestions are in italics.

LESSON I.—What is the other name for the World?—What does Geography mean?—What shape is the Earth?—*Show the children clearly what a globe is.*—What is the surface?—Tell me the names of some kinds of plants.—Some kinds of animals.—Do you know how water differs from land?—What does the shore mean?—Have you ever seen the sea?—What are boats and ships for?—*Show how they differ, and ask if any child has seen them.*—*Look*

---

* Some of the lessons, generally easier in their nature, are longer than others ; such lessons can be divided at the teacher's discretion into two parts.

SHIP, STEAMER, AND BOAT.

4. We have to give different names to the divisions of land and water, so that we may be able to describe them exactly.

A large flat piece of land, where we can walk for miles, from the middle, in any direction, without coming to a rise in the ground, is called a *plain.*

A plain is a large flat piece of land.

5. Now there is a great extent of the land where we find that the ground slopes, and gradually becomes raised higher than the level parts around it. We have to climb when we want to go up rising ground; and if it is easy to climb, and not very high, we call it a *hill.* But if it be much taller, and harder to ascend, we call this high land a *mountain.*

The higher parts of the land are called mountains and hills.

6. There are mountains in some parts of the world several miles in height. The air is always colder at the top of a mountain than below, and often its upper portion is covered with snow all the year round. The *summit* is the name given to the top of a mountain, and the lowest part is called its *base.*

LESSON II.

1. About the Land.—There are a few mountains which cast out smoke and fire at their summits. Often, too, a stream of melted rocks runs down their sides, burning and destroying everything it touches. These burning mountains are called *volcanoes.* The terrible stream they send forth is named *lava.* The lava has been known to bury whole towns, and nearly all the people who lived in them. Fortunately for us, we have no burning mountains in our country.

VOLCANO.

at the illustration.—What are sailors ?—*Explain the word division.*—What is a plain ?—Is there any plain in this neighbourhood ?—*Speak of the Sahara and the Prairies.*—What is a hill ?—What is a mountain ?—Have you ever seen any hills ?—Why is it tiring to climb up anything ?—What is snow ?—At what time of the year does it fall in England ?—What name is given to the top of a mountain ?

A volcano is a burning mountain, sending forth fire, smoke, and lava.

2. A mountain sometimes stands by itself, but more usually it is joined with many others into a kind of row, called a *chain* or *range*. Sometimes a number of mountains are simply placed near one another, without being in one line. Then they form a *group*.

3. If the top of a mountain is sharp and pointed, it is called a *peak*. If any part of its sides is almost like a wall, so steep that it cannot be climbed without great danger, we say that it is a *precipice*.

4. The hollows that lie between ranges or groups of mountains are called *valleys*. Some small valleys are called in England *dales*. These hollows are often very beautiful and fertile.

5. Some countries are low and almost flat. Others, again, are full of mountains and valleys, and here and there we find large plains raised up between the mountains, high above the rest of the country. These flat lands, which might be said to be lifted up just like a table above a floor, are called *table-lands*.

A level land, raised high up above the earth's surface, is called a table-land.

LESSON III.—(Parts I. and II.)

(PART I.)—1. **About the Water on the Land.**—We must now learn something about the water on the earth's surface.

You have all seen rain falling and snow melting. You have observed, too, how wet the ground becomes after a heavy shower. A great deal of water is soaked up by the earth, and sinks down deeper and deeper. By-and-by some clay or rock stops its downward movement, and the water gradually gathers below the surface, or, if the land is sloping, flows out to the open air. If more water still continues to come, and it can neither sink lower nor flow out along a slope, it must of course rise *up*. So, in one way or other, the water at last springs out on the surface of the ground, and it will do so as long as fresh supplies of water are added.

LESSON II.—What is a volcano?—*Tell them where the fire comes from.*—Does the lava do any harm?—*Say something about the story of Pompeii.*—Are there any burning mountains in England?—If mountains are placed near one another, but not in a single line, what are they called?—What is a *range?*—Draw a *peak* on your slate.—*Show them by familiar illustrations what a precipice is.*—What is a valley?—*Explain the word fertile.*—Why would you expect a valley or dale to be more fertile than a mountain?—*If possible, give the children examples in your own neighbourhood, and try to make them think.*—What difference is there between a table-land and a plain?—*Tell them something of the flats of Holland; also of the table-lands in the Andes.*

LESSON III.—Where does the rain come from?—Have you ever seen snow and ice?—Tell me what they are like.—When does the snow on the ground melt?—What is a spring? How are springs formed?—What is a well?—What sorts of springs are there?—*Tell them of*

A place where water flows out of the earth is called a spring.

People have very often to dig down into the earth some way before they can meet with a spring. They make what is called a *well* for this purpose. But sometimes, when the ground is hilly, a spring rushes forth at the surface with much force.

2. The water, when it bubbles out of the ground at a spring, is usually cold and pleasant to drink. Many springs are, however, known to be quite hot, and these are generally believed to come from a great depth. Some, again, which we call *mineral springs*, taste of iron, sulphur, and other things.

SPRING AND RILL.

3. Water will always flow downwards, and so, when it comes out of a spring on a hill-side, it runs away towards the plains or valleys. As it passes on, it meets with the water coming from other springs, and thus a little *rill* or *streamlet* is formed. This streamlet may be very tiny at first, but it joins others after a while, and a single *brook* or *rivulet* is made. Then, further down the valley, or along the plain, this brook meets with a brook that has come from some other place, and the waters of the two at once unite, flowing along henceforth as a single stream. Thus a *river* is made.

A river is a large stream of water formed by several smaller streams joining together.

(PART II.)—4. There is no difference between a rill, a brook, and a river, you see, except in size. A river is simply a large brook, and a brook is a large rill. Many rivers are very large. There are, in some parts of the world, rivers several miles in width.

5. When the land slopes greatly all running water flows quickly, but through plains it usually goes slower. A river's path is called a *course*, and the hollow ground through which it flows is said to be its *bed*. The edges of the land bordering a river on either side are its *banks*. The banks and bed have been formed by the action of the river water, which can cut a way for itself through earth and even through rocks in time.

the Harrogate and Bath springs, and say something about the Geysers.—What way does water always flow?—If you were near running water, how would you know which way the land sloped?—What is a rill?—What other name have you for a brook?—What is a river? —Name some rivers you have seen.—Give the Amazon as an example of a great river.—What use can men make of running water?—What is the real difference between rills, brooks, and

6. A great river has its branches, or *tributaries*, spread over a large tract of country, so the water in it comes from very many different places, some far distant from others. Very often what seems to be a large river may simply be the branch or tributary of a still larger one; but all rivers at last fall into a greater body of water, through what is called a *mouth*. This mouth is really the end of the river, and if we were to go up the banks of a stream as far as we possibly could, we should at last come to its beginning or *source*. The source is always at a greater height than the land near the river's mouth.

A river must have its source in a place higher than its mouth. It flows along a course, and its bed is bordered by banks.

7. When the course of a river is steep, and the stream rushes along so violently that boats cannot go up, it is said to form a *rapid;* but when the waters suddenly fall down over lofty rocks, a *waterfall* is produced.

There is a wonderful waterfall, called Niagara, where the whole of the waters of an enormous river suddenly fall down a great height, more than twenty times the height of a full-grown man. This waterfall makes a noise as loud as thunder, that can be heard many miles away.

FALLS OF NIAGARA.

LESSON IV.

1. More about the Water on the Land.—When rain falls heavily, or when snow melts, the waters of a river become higher, and they may rise over

rivers ?— *Explain the words* BANKS, BED, COURSE, *and* TRIBUTARY.—*Show the power of water in transporting earth, gravel, and stones.*—If a river-bed slopes greatly, how does the water run ?—In a flat country do the rivers run quickly ?—Why must the waters of a great river come from very many different places ?—What is the mouth of a river ?—What do we call the place where a stream begins ?—Which is higher, the source or the mouth ?—Why ?—What is a rapid ?—What use can be made of rapids and waterfalls ?—Are there any water-mills near us ?—What do you know about Niagara ?—How high is it ?

LESSON IV.—Why does a river sometimes flow over its banks ?—*Say something about*

the banks and flood the country around.   After many days of warm, dry weather, a river loses a great deal of its water.   You might then almost walk across many a stream which is wide and deep at other times of the year.

2. Large hollows or valleys sometimes become filled with water and form lakes.

A lake is a piece of water lying in hollow ground, and surrounded by land.

3. Some rivers have their sources in lakes, others end in them, and others pass through them.   A small lake, with calm, still waters, is a *pond* or *pool*.   In some very warm countries there are shallow lakes which become almost dry

RIVER AND LAKE.

when rain ceases falling, and again spread out when wet weather begins.   Some lakes, too, are being slowly filled up by mud brought into them by a river. There are, however, many large and deep lakes, on which boats and even ships may sail.   The water of most lakes is fresh, but in some it is very salt.

4. To show you how large a lake sometimes is, I may tell you that, in a great country called North America, there is a fresh-water lake which is more than half as large as England.   And in another part of the world, called Asia, there is

the inundations of the Nile, and the meaning of "Cast thy bread upon the waters" (Eccl. xi. 1).—At what time of the year is a river fullest in England?—When is it lowest?—You might mention here the temporary rivers of Australia and South Africa.—What is a lake?—Are rivers ever connected with lakes?—Do you know of any pond?—Have you ever seen water-lilies growing?—Tell about the great shallow lakes in Central Africa, also speak of the Dead Sea and Lake Titicaca.—Are there any very great lakes?—What is the size of the largest salt-water lake?—The lakes in Par. 4 are Lake Superior and the Caspian Sea.—Explain the word SCENERY, *and speak of the more celebrated English, Scotch, or Irish lakes.—What is a marsh?—Give me two other names for it.—Is there much difference between a marsh and a lake?—You might here tell the children what peat is, and say something about the Fens, or the Irish bogs.*

one still greater. This is a salt lake, and the whole of England would not cover one half of it. In our country none of the lakes are very large, but some of them have beautiful scenery, especially when they are surrounded by mountains.

MOUNTAIN LAKE.

5. A *marsh, swamp,* or *bog* is a piece of wet, soft ground. If it were covered deeper with water, it would be a lake.

LESSON V.

1. About the Ocean.—I have told you already that the whole of the earth's surface, or outside, is covered with land and water. But there is far more water than land. Indeed, the land only covers about a fourth of the globe, while all the rest is water. For there is three times as much water as land.

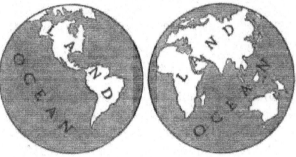

WESTERN HEMISPHERE. EASTERN HEMISPHERE.

2. One enormous sheet of water surrounds all the land. Here is a picture of both sides of the globe. If you look at it, you will see how little land there is, and how great is the extent of the water.

3. This vast extent of water is what we call the *Ocean* or *Sea.* The edge of the land along it is called the *sea-shore* or *coast.* Perhaps you have been beside the sea, and have seen its great waves, and watched the ships sailing over it. No matter in what part of the world you might

LESSON V.—With what is the Earth's surface covered ?—How much land is there ?— How much water ?—*Show the children a globe, if possible, and point out to them the water and the land. This will explain the subject better than a flat map.*—What is the coast ?—Who has ever seen the sea ?—Tell me what you can about it.—How is it that if you walk in a straight line far enough you must at last come to the sea ?—What can be seen when one is

SAILING-SHIP.

be, if you were only to walk on and on in one straight line, you would at last come to this great sea or *ocean*, for you know now that it surrounds all the land. When sailors go out in their ships and begin to cross the ocean, they soon lose sight of the shore they have sailed from. Then perhaps for days, or even weeks, they may see nothing from their ship but the sky above and the deep waters below, except when they happen to pass another vessel. After a while, however, they begin to observe a dark line appearing before them, where the sky and the sea seem to meet. As they sail on, it becomes clearer, wider, and higher, and they find that it is the shore of another country.

The Sea or Ocean is an immense extent of salt water surrounding all the land.

4. The waters of the Ocean are deep blue or green in colour, and are very salt, and even bitter, to the taste. Sometimes the sea is almost as calm as a pond ; but when the winds blow, great waves arise, and many vessels are wrecked and their sailors drowned. A seaman's life is a very dangerous one. Yet we could not do without ships. I will leave you to guess why.

5. Though the Ocean is *really* one great water, the land is so placed in it as to divide it into several large parts, which have different names. The largest of these is called the *Pacific Ocean*, the next in size is the *Atlantic Ocean*. The other oceans are the *Indian*, the *Southern*, the *Arctic*, and the *Antarctic*.

LESSON VI.

1. **About the Divisions of the Ocean.**—I have said that the great Ocean itself is generally called *the Sea*. But the word *sea* is also used to mean a smaller division of water than an ocean. A *sea* is very often partly surrounded by land.

A sea is a large division of water, but it is smaller than an ocean.

far out on the Ocean ?—Tell me what sailors see when they begin to approach land ?—What is the great Sea or Ocean ?—What colour are its waters ?—Are they pleasant to taste ?—Would they quench your thirst ?—*Tell about the fish of the sea, the whale, the coral animal, &c.*—Is the sea ever still ?—When is it rough ?—What often happens during storms ?—Why is a sailor's life dangerous ?—Why could we not do without ships ?—Give me the names of the six great divisions of the Ocean.—Which is the largest ?—Which is the second in size ?

LESSON VI.—What two meanings has the word *sea* ?—Tell me what a sea is.—What is a gulf ?—What is a bay ?—Draw a picture of a gulf and a bay on your slate.—What are

2. A long narrow piece of water running into the land is named a *gulf*.

3. A *bay* is another portion of water partly surrounded by land, but it is not so long and narrow as a *gulf* is. Sometimes it is merely a small bend of

SEA, BAY, CHANNEL, AND HARBOUR.

the sea into the land. There are large gulfs and small gulfs, large bays and small bays. The difference between the words bay and gulf is really trifling. They are both bodies of water more or less surrounded by land.

A division of the water extending into the land, and smaller than a sea, is called a gulf or a bay.

4. If two seas are joined together by a narrow strip of water it is named a *strait*, and if it be wider it is a *channel*.

Straits and channels are passages which join two seas.

5. When the waters of a small, sheltered bay are calm and deep, so that a ship can anchor there in safety, this place is said to be a *harbour*. A bay nearly shut in by the land has far smaller waves than the sea outside.

6. Sometimes a river enters the sea by a long deep mouth, almost like a gulf, up which the sea waters can pass for some distance. This is an *estuary* or *firth*. In our country there are several estuaries.

LESSON VII.—(Parts I. and II.)

(PART I.)—**1. How Rain is made, and why the Sea does not over-flow.**—Now that we have learnt a good deal about water, we must soon pass on

straits and channels ?—What is the difference between them ?—What is the meaning of a ship *anchoring?*—Have you ever seen an anchor ?—Who can draw a picture of one ?—What is the use of a harbour ?—What makes its waters still ?—Why cannot the large sea waves pass into the harbour ?—What do you sometimes find at the mouth of a river ?—Does any one of you know the difference between an estuary and a gulf ?—Would the water of an estuary be very salt ?—Another name for estuary.—*You might tell them something about the estuaries of the Severn, the Thames, and the Humber, or of the Shannon, or about the Firths of Forth and Clyde.*

B

to other matters. But, before doing so, I should like to ask you two questions, which some of you have perhaps been thinking about already. If so many rivers are continually pouring water into the sea, how is it that the sea does not at last get so full as to flow over the land? And, again, where does the rain come from that has to supply such an enormous number of springs, brooks, rivers, and lakes? Well, I must try to explain this to you, but perhaps you will have to wait till you are a little older and wiser before you can understand the subject fully.

2. Have you ever seen a puddle left in the road after a heavy shower in summer, and noticed how quickly it dries up when the sun shines out again, even where the ground is hard and the water cannot sink into it? Or, again, do you remember how I told you that in some warm countries the lakes and rivers become almost dry when the weather is very hot? And surely every one of you has observed, too, how quickly wet things become dry in the bright sunbeams. *Where does all this water go?*

3. *The warm rays of the sun* draw it up, and change it into "vapour." We cannot see this vapour. It rises from the surface of the water and mixes with the invisible air around us; but it is there all the same, and it is constantly going up from the sea and all other bodies of water. By-and-by it reaches the upper and colder regions of the air, and becomes visible in the shape of those beautiful clouds above us, which have so many strange forms and colours. Not one drop of water changed into vapour by the sun's heat is wasted. The clouds let it fall down in rain; the springs take it up and pass it to the brooks, and rivers, and lakes; it thence flows into the great ocean, and from the ocean it rises once more into the air, as vapour, to feed the clouds. If a drop of water could speak, what a wonderful story it might tell!

(PART II.)—4. Have you not all seen a rainbow? This beautiful coloured arch is often formed during a heavy shower, or afterwards, when the sun begins to shine out again on the dark rain-clouds. It is always seen *opposite* to the sun.

5. Some countries have heavy rains during one part of the year, and dry weather through the rest of it. In our land rain may come at any season. But there are some unfortunate places in the world where rain is almost always falling; and, what is still worse, rain *never falls at all* in some others. The

LESSON VII.—Why does the sea not get too full and overflow?—What is vapour?—Can you see it?—What forms the clouds?—How do you know that the Sun is always drawing up water?—Is there any water wasted?—Why not?—Now tell me, if you can, how the waters of the earth are always changing about.—What is a rainbow?—In what part of the sky is it seen?—Tell me how rain falls in different parts of the world.—Does it rain very often here?—Which months are generally the wettest?—*Something might here be said of the great rainfalls on the West and South-West coasts of the United Kingdom, and the comparative*

land is then so dry that hardly any plants will grow on it, and its animals are as few as its plants. It becomes a terrible *desert.*

CARAVAN CROSSING THE DESERT.

A land without rain, where very few plants and animals can live, is called a desert.

7. When the air grows very cold, and what we call *frosty weather* sets in, water becomes hard and solid. It is then said to be *frozen.* At this time the raindrops are turned as they fall into soft, white flakes of *snow,* or even into little solid pellets, called *hail,* which may do a great deal of injury to crops and animals. The still water in the lakes and pools becomes coated over with a glass-like substance named *ice,* and if the cold is very severe even the running streams may be frozen as well. It requires very cold weather to freeze the salt waters of the sea.

ICE AND SNOW.

8. Snow usually falls in winter, but hail will fall even in summer, if the air should have grown very cold. In some lands where there is little warmth in the air the snow lies on the ground for a great part of the year, and, as I have already told you, on the

dryness of the Eastern counties.—What is a desert?—Why can few plants live there?—Would you expect to meet many men or animals in a desert?—*Good examples of deserts are Sahara, Gobi, and part of Peru.*—What do you mean by frosty weather?—What is snow?—What is hail?—Does hail ever fall in summer?—If frost comes, what sort of water will freeze first?—What water freezes last?—Are there any places where snow and ice always remain?—What is a thaw?—Why is it disagreeable to go out of doors when it is thawing?—*Give an easy account of icebergs, the Alpine snows, avalanches, and glaciers; the St. Bernard dogs; Laplanders and their reindeer.*—*Take care to use simple language in your narratives.*

tops of many mountains the ice and snow never melt. You all know how disagreeable it is to go out in winter if the weather is getting warmer, and the ice and snow are melting. We then say that a *thaw* has set in.

LESSON VIII.

1. About the Shapes of the Land.—If you look once more at the little picture of the World that I showed you, you will see how very uneven in form the land is.

The very large masses of land (one of which you will notice in each half of the picture) are called *continents*.

A continent is the largest division of land.

2. There are two great continents. The wider and larger one is called the "Old World," because it was the only part of the Earth that people knew about till four hundred years ago, when a brave and clever man, named Christopher Columbus, sailed boldly out on the ocean, farther than any one had ever ventured before. He believed that he should find new land, and he was right, for at last he came to a great country which no one in the Old World had ever heard of before. We call this large continent the "New World," or *America*. You observe that it is very long, but not nearly so wide as the Old World. I dare say, too, you see how it is almost divided in the middle.

3. Sometimes large divisions of a continent are called continents as well, just as large portions of the ocean are called oceans. But there are, in reality, only *two* great continents.

A piece of land entirely surrounded by water is called an island.

4. One large island, named *Australia*, which you see in the corner of the picture of the World, is of such great size that it is often spoken of as a continent. There are very many islands in the World; some stand alone, and others are placed closely together in an *archipelago*. We live on an island in a group called the British Islands, but the principal islands in that group are few in number.

An archipelago is a very large group of islands.

5. When a piece of land juts out into the sea, and is *nearly* surrounded

LESSON VIII.—[*Before asking any questions hang up a large map of the world.*]—*Explain* "*uneven.*"—What is a continent ?—How many large continents are in the picture ?—Show me them.—Point out the Old World.—Why is it called "old" ?—Who was Christopher Columbus ?—*Let them see whence and whither he sailed.*—What other name has the New World ?—What difference is there in the shape of the two continents ?—Is the word *continent* used to mean anything else ?—What is an island ?—What large island is often called a continent ?—What do we call a large number of islands grouped together ?—Can

by water, we call it a *peninsula.* The word peninsula means " almost an island." It is curious to notice that nearly all the peninsulas of the world point the same way.

6. The very end of a piece of land which stretches out into the sea is called a *cape.* It has many other names besides, such as *point, head, promontory.* You can very easily show me many capes in the little picture of the World of which I have so often spoken.

7. If two large portions of land are joined together by one little strip stretched between them, that little strip is called an *isthmus.* Look at the picture of the New World, and you will notice a good example of an isthmus at the place where it is so nearly divided.

An isthmus is a narrow strip of land joining two larger portions of land.

CONTINENT, ISLAND, ARCHIPELAGO, PENINSULA, CAPE, AND ISTHMUS.

LESSON IX.—(Parts I. and II.)

(PART I.)—**1. About the Planets, the Sun, and the Moon.**—You have been told in your very first lesson that the Earth, on the surface of which we live, is an immense ball or globe.

If you were to throw an orange up ever so high, you know it would fall down again to the ground. But suppose it were possible for it to remain in the air *without falling,* it would then give you a sort of very small idea of the way in which the Earth is hung up in space, although there seems to be nothing to hold it.

you tell me the name of any island ?—What is a peninsula ?—What does the word *peninsula* mean ?—*Point out to the children the common southern direction of peninsulas.*—What is a cape ?—Show me some capes.—Are there any other names for a cape ?—Give the exact meaning of isthmus.—Where do you see an isthmus on this picture ?—Show it to me.

LESSON IX.—[*This lesson is necessarily a little difficult and lengthy, so that it may be found advisable to divide it.*]—What shape is the Earth ?—Give me some idea of the way in which the Earth is placed in the sky.—What is it that holds it up ?—What great ball has

2. And yet *there is* something which keeps the Earth in its place. When you are older, and are better able to learn a thing that is too hard for children's understanding, you will then hear of a wonderful power, called *attraction*, which compels that great round ball, the Earth, to stay within a certain distance of a far greater ball, the Sun. The Earth cannot "fall," for the attraction of the Sun is always acting upon it, so that it can never go farther away.

3. The Sun looks very small indeed when seen in our sky, but that is simply because we are at an enormous distance from it. It is really *far* larger than the Earth, and learned men have found out that while the Sun is itself at rest the Earth is always moving round it.

4. It will very likely surprise you to hear all this. You have seen the Sun rising every day, going across the sky, and then setting in the evening; so perhaps you thought that *it* moved, and that the Earth remained still all the time. But if you did, you were altogether mistaken. The Sun always stays in one place, and it is our own world, with all its seas, its lands, and its people, that is ever travelling on through the sky. Round and round the

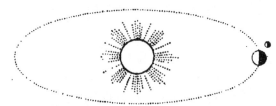

THE EARTH REVOLVING ROUND THE SUN.

Sun, in a journey that ends not, keeping to the one path, the Earth moves on, and will move on for ever. It travels once round this circle in just about one year (or 365 days). So we say that

The Earth takes a year to move once round the Sun.

(PART. II.)—5. The Earth is not the only great ball that revolves round the Sun. Many of the little twinkling stars are worlds, rolling on for ever just like ours. Some are nearer the Sun than we are, others farther away; and if we look up above, night after night, we can see them passing slowly from one part of the sky to another, as they go along on their wonderful, eternal paths through the heavens. We call all those stars that move round the Sun *planets*, and our Earth is a planet too.

the Earth attracted towards it ?—Can the Sun and Earth go farther away from each other, or approach nearer ?—*A black board will help you to explain this.—Or a useful illustration might be made with two balls of different size ; for example, a globe and an orange.*—Why does the Sun seem so small to us ?—Which moves, Sun or Earth ?—How long does the Earth take to go round the Sun ?—What do we get from the Sun ?—*There should be no difficulty in explaining to intelligent children why it is that the air does not get hotter as we climb higher up on the Earth's surface.*—Are there any other bodies revolving round the Sun ?—What name have they ?—*The teacher should, if at all possible, show his children, some starry night, the planets then visible, and point out a few of the fixed stars ; such a lesson is*

6. By far the greater number of stars, however, are something very different. They twinkle just as brightly, *but they never change their places.* Every clear night we see them where we saw them before, and so people call them *fixed stars.* You will wonder when I tell you that they are so very, very far away that we can hardly form an idea of their great distance from us, and it is not unlikely that many of them are themselves suns, with planets like our Earth ever whirling round them.

When we consider these wonderful things, we should also turn our minds to the boundless power and goodness of that great God who made them all, and we should thank Him heartily for the gracious care which He bestows on every one of us.

7. Some of you are perhaps thinking about the Moon now, and wondering what *it* may be. Well, the Moon is neither a planet nor a fixed star, but it is a follower of our own Earth. Just as the Earth moves round the Sun, so does the Moon move round the Earth. It requires a month to go once round this path, and it is a smaller body than the Earth, and much less distant from it than the Earth is from the Sun. I have not time to tell you now why you see the full Moon at one time, and at another only the half of it, or even the quarter. You shall learn all about that by-and-by, and I have so much to say about the Earth itself that I must go on to other matters.

Remember what you have just learned :

The Earth and several of the Stars are Planets, moving round the Sun.

Most of the Stars are said to be fixed, for we always see them in the same places. They are very much farther from the Earth than the Planets and Sun are.

The Moon is a globe that revolves round our Earth.

LESSON X.—(Parts I. and II.)

(Part I.)—**1. About the Roundness of the Earth.**—I have now told you several times that the Earth is a ball or globe, but I think you would all like to have some *proofs* of its roundness.

---

easy to give, besides being very interesting and instructive.—What is the difference between fixed stars and planets ?—How does the Moon move ?—In what time does it go once round the Earth ?—*You can, perhaps, explain simply the phenomena of quarter and half Moon, but it is not absolutely necessary to do so here.*—*Interesting matter might be added on the Moon's volcanoes, the Sun's composition, Jupiter's moons, Saturn's rings, &c.—But do not give too much information at once.*—*Vide* "Lockyer's Elementary Astronomy."

LESSON X.—PART I.—How do we know that the Earth is round ?—If I were walking

There are a great many of these proofs, some of them a little hard to understand at first, but others easy enough. I will mention two.

2. Because both the ocean and the land are curved, a sailor can only see the tops of the mountains when he is coming first in sight of a country. After a while he sees the lower parts, but the shore last of all. And so, too, if you were standing on the sea-beach and looking at a distant vessel sailing towards

you, the first thing you could observe would most certainly be the tops of the masts. Then by-and-by the sails would come into view, and lastly the hull. If, however, the ship were sailing *away*, the hull would disappear first, then the sails, and at last the very tops of the masts.

3. Many people have travelled round the Earth. By going onwards in a straight course for a long time they have at last returned to the very place from which they at first started.

4. You see, then, that the Earth must be of a round shape. It is hardly *quite* round, but is more like an orange than a ball, for it is very slightly flattened at two opposite points. These points are called the *poles*.

The Poles are the two opposite points where the Earth is slightly flattened.

I want you particularly to remember what the poles are, for I have more to tell you about them.

5. You have heard how the Earth moves round the Sun. You shall now learn about *another* way in which it turns, that is, *on itself*.

I can give you a pretty good idea of what I mean if you will take an orange and a knitting-needle (or any piece of straight wire). The orange is very like the World in its round shape, flattened at both the ends, or " poles," so that this will do for a little model of it. Now push the needle straight through the orange, passing it in at the little black spot on the top, and bringing it out exactly on the opposite side. If you turn the orange round and round on the

up a round-topped hill, and a boy came up the other side, what part of him should I see first ?—And if I were on a sea-shore, looking out for a ship sailing towards me, what part of it should I expect to see first ?—What part last ?—Why ?—Do you know why we can see much further from the top of a tower than from the bottom of it ?—*This the teacher can easily explain by a sketch on the black board.—Show also why a sailor goes up to the topmast to look for land.*—Have people ever travelled round the Earth ?—*Show this on the globe.*—What are the poles ?—Find me the poles on this globe.—You know that the Earth goes round the

needle, you will easily understand what I mean by saying that the earth turns on itself.

6. Of course there is no such needle in the Earth, nor any other *real* line for it to turn on; but we must imagine one, and call it the  *axis.* The axis passes through the middle of the Earth, going from one pole straight to the other, so that the poles are simply its ends. One pole is named the North Pole, and the other the South Pole.

The middle of the Earth is its Centre.

The Axis of the Earth is the line on which it turns.

The North and South Poles are at the ends of the axis.

7. The Earth makes one turn on its axis in twenty-four hours.

(PART II.*)—8. I think this will be a good time for you to learn one or two things more about the Earth's form and size that I have not yet told you.

The Circumference of the Earth is the distance round it.

The distance round the Earth is very nearly the same in whatever direction it is measured; only, it must divide the surface of the Earth into halves. Now if you cut a piece of string just long enough to go once round a ball, so that exactly *half* the ball may be on each side of the string, you will find that the same piece of string will also go round the ball in any other direction, and that half the ball will, in every case, be on each side of it. You know how easy it is to cut an orange in two, and that a cut straight through the middle, no matter what way the orange is turned, will divide it into exact halves. The line round the edge of the cut half of the orange, if measured, would give you its circumference.

The circumference of the Earth is about 25,000 miles in length.

Half the Earth is called a Hemisphere.

The distance through the centre of the Earth from surface to surface is its diameter.

Sun once in the year. But what other way does it also turn?—What is the axis?—Is it a *real* line?—What do I mean by the centre of the Earth?—Name the two poles.—In what time does the Earth turn once on its axis?

PART. II.—What is the circumference of the Earth?—*Measure the circumference of your school globe in illustration, and show that the distance is the same in whatever way it is measured.*—How much of the Earth is on each side of a line drawn in this way?—How long is the Earth's circumference?—What is a hemisphere?—a diameter?—*See that the spelling of*

---

* It will perhaps be found best to hear Part II. of Lesson X. as a separate lesson.

9. The axis of which I have been speaking would, if measured, give the diameter of the Earth. But all lines drawn through a ball are the same in length when they pass through the middle (or *centre*) of the ball. If you pierce an orange with a knitting-needle in several directions, taking care that it passes through the centre, you will find that the length of the part of the needle *inside* the orange is always about the same.

It is the *diameter* of the orange. You surely know now what a diameter is.

The Earth's diameter is nearly 8000 miles in length.

10. The last thing I have to tell you in this lesson is the meaning of a word that you will frequently meet with—*Equator.*

A line supposed to be drawn round the world, at exactly the same distance from each pole, is called the Equator.

Let us take the orange once more and see if we can find an equator on it.

Just half-way between the points where the needle passes through it (that is to say, its poles) we notice that the orange is thickest. If we were to draw a line here round the orange as it turned on the needle, we should have a circle which would give us a good idea of what the Equator is. You see it is the largest circle that could be drawn straight round the orange, so as to divide it into two equal parts, with a pole exactly at the top of each. Any other circles drawn straight across the orange would grow smaller and smaller as they approached the poles.

The Equator divides the Earth into two Hemispheres, the Northern and the Southern.

The Equator is sometimes simply called *the line.*

---

these words is known.—If I were to plunge a knitting-needle through the middle of an orange, what part of the needle would show the diameter of the orange?—How long is the Earth's diameter?—What do you call the line which is supposed to be drawn round the Earth exactly at the same distance from each pole?—Tell me the name given to each half of the Earth as divided by the Equator.—*With the aid of a halved orange and the school globe, explain to the children, in simple words, the meaning of* EQUATOR, CIRCUMFERENCE, AXIS, *and* POLE. *Also, show that no circle can be larger than the Equator.*—The Equator is often called by what short name?—*Explain* "crossing the line."

LESSON XI.

1. More about the Motions of the Earth.—In the last lessons you have learned, besides other things, that the Earth moves round the Sun once in 365 days (a year), and that it turns upon itself once in twenty-four hours (a day and a night).

2. We know, then, that the Earth has two motions, which are always going on at the same time—namely, a motion round its own axis, and a motion round the Sun. I think you will not find it hard to understand how these can happen together. It is surely easy enough for anything to be moving onwards, and yet to be turning round and round on itself all the time. Just look, for instance, how a carriage wheel keeps turning as it runs along a road; or, still better, observe your top as it goes rapidly whirling when it is spun, both turning on itself and making a sort of circle on the ground at the same moment.

3. It is indeed curious to think of our world as rushing through the sky with all its inhabitants, and even its very air and clouds, on its long year's journey round the Sun. Even since we read these last words it has gone many, many miles further, and it will not return to the same place in the sky for twelve months hence! And while it is thus rushing onward, it is rapidly turning on itself, so rapidly that both the ground under our feet and the house in which we are sitting are now more than ten miles distant from the point at which they were a minute ago, and it will take twenty-four hours for the Earth to turn completely round and bring them back to their present position.

MOONLIGHT SCENE.

4. About Day and Night.—It is the turning of the Earth on its axis that causes day and night. Almost all the light in the sky comes from the Sun. The very Moon only shines by the help of that Sun, which, even when we cannot see it, is still sending out its light and heat. So it brightens up the dark Moon, and enables it to give us a feeble light during our night-time. You

Lesson XI.—How many motions has the Earth?—Do the two motions go on together?—Do you know anything else that moves in this way, both rolling round on itself and going onward at the same time?—When will the earth have come back again to the place in the sky at which it is at this very moment?—And how much time will the Earth require to spin once round on itself, so as to bring the ground we are standing on back to its present position?—*Explain carefully with a chalk sketch and the globe.*—What causes day and night?—From what do we get our light?—How does the moon receive its light?—

all know how cold and pale the moonbeams are, compared with the rich, warm rays of the Sun itself.

The Moon's light is only light reflected from the Sun.

5. You are well aware that it is day-time when the Sun is shining over our heads, and that at night the darkness begins and daylight goes away. It will not take much thinking to see that the Sun can only shine on that side of the world which is turned *towards* it; and, of course, as there is no light to be got

elsewhere, the opposite side of the Earth is at that time perfectly dark, or, at all events, has nothing more than the moonbeams shining on it.

6. Now if the Earth were standing still, the people who lived in the countries on the side opposite the Sun would have nothing but day, and the poor people on the other side of the world would have one long, endless night. But, since the Earth is always turning on itself, every part of it is brought round gradually to the light, and again passes into the darkness. Thus day and night come to all parts of the world.

7. I am sure that everyone of you now knows what "sunrise" and "sunset" mean, and could tell me that when the Sun is *rising* in the early morning *we* are moving into its light, but that when it is *setting* the part of the earth on which we live is passing away from it.

The daily motion of the Earth on its axis gives us day and night.

LESSON XII.—(Parts I. and II.)

(PART I.)—1. **About the Seasons, and more about Day and Night.**
—In countries which, like ours, are about equally removed from the Equator, where the hot weather lasts all the year round, and from the Pole, where

If you can darken the room, you can easily demonstrate the phenomena of day and night by means of a lamp, a globe (for the Earth), and an orange (for the Moon).—Which side of the Earth does the Sun light up ?—Why is it that half the world is in constant darkness, while the other half is always lit up ?—Does the sun really *rise* in the morning and *set* at night ?—Tell me, once more, what gives us day and night.

LESSON XII.—[*Before commencing, explain Seasons, Hemisphere, Equator, Poles, Temperate. See also if the children understand the two motions of the Earth.*]—What is a season ?—How many seasons are there in England ?—Name them.—Tell me what you see in Spring,

the cold is always intense, the year is divided into four parts or *Seasons*, in each of which the weather is different. We call the Seasons *Spring, Summer, Autumn,* and *Winter.*

PLOUGHING.

2. In *Spring* the weather is generally mild and agreeable. Buds and flowers come out, bright green leaves begin to appear on the trees, the birds sing and build their nests, and though there are showers the sun shines out nearly every day. The farmers then sow their seeds, and plants grow quickly.

3. Next we have *Summer.* The sunbeams are very hot and powerful now; the trees are all covered with leaves, though they do not look half as bright as they did in the Spring-time. But there are very many flowers in bloom;. fruits are beginning to ripen; the nights are short and the days long; and so Summer is a very pleasant season of the year. The hay is cut, and the corn-fields begin to get yellow.

HAYMAKING.

4. *Autumn* comes afterwards. The days are growing shorter and the nights longer, but it is very hot at noon. Grain and fruits are ripe. The harvest takes place, and then we see the leaves on the trees turning from green into beautiful shades of brown and red and yellow. At last they begin to fall, littering the garden paths, and lying thickly under the boughs in the woods. Another season is at hand.

5. This is the fourth and last one —*Winter.* The days are very short now and the nights very long. The

HARVESTING.

in Summer, in Autumn, in Winter.—When do farmers sow seeds ?—When do they reap their harvest ?—When are the days longest ?—When shortest ?—When does very cold weather

Sun shines sometimes, and looks very red, but gives very little warmth. You never see it high up in the sky as you did in Summer. The weather becomes extremely cold. Snow falls often in beautiful soft flakes, which soon cover the earth with a thick wrapper of pure white. The brooks and ponds are all choked up with ice, and people have to be warmly muffled when they go out of doors. The trees have lost all their leaves (except some of them, called evergreens), and their naked branches will look sad and dark till the bright Spring returns again. *(See Illustration on page 19.)*

(PART II.)—6. Thus every year come Spring, Summer, Autumn, and Winter in the happy land where we live. And, as I have told you, these seasons occur in all other countries where the heat and cold are not extremely great at any time of the year. Such countries are said to be *temperate* countries.

7. But there are parts of the world which are exceedingly hot at all times, while in some others the cold lasts through the greater part of the year. The cold countries have a very short Summer and a very long Winter, while the only difference of weather in the hot lands is a wet season and a dry one.

8. The hottest lands are near the Equator. Just on the Equator day and night are always exactly equal in length—twelve hours each.

9. The coldest lands are about the Poles, and in them also the day is as long as the night. But there is only *one* long day and *one* long night through the whole year, each lasting for six months. If it were possible for you to live at the North Pole you would have to go to bed by daylight all through the Summer,

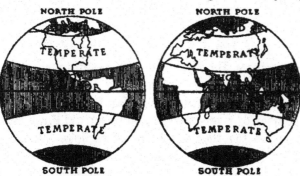

DIFFERENT REGIONS OF TEMPERATURE.

and in Winter you would never see the Sun at all.

10. In the parts of the world between the hot Equator and the cold Poles the length of day and night is different at different times of the year. Here are the *temperate* countries, where the *four* seasons that you have heard about come each year.

come?—What may you expect to see in Winter?—Name some trees that keep their leaves all Winter.—Now by what name do we call countries in which there are these four seasons?—Show me some such countries on the map or globe.—*Let the teacher constantly refer to the globe in this lesson, as its round surface will illustrate the subject better than any flat map.*—Are there any countries hotter than ours?—Where?—And are not some other parts of the world much colder than England?—Where are the cold countries?—How long are the days and nights at the Equator?—At the Poles?—Would it be dark when you went to bed in Summer at the North Pole?—How long would your night last there in Winter-time?—Have we always short nights and long days in England?—At what time of the year, then, are the

11. Now there are two sets of temperate countries—one in the Northern Hemisphere, one in the Southern. And no doubt you will think it a strange thing that when it is Winter in the one it is Summer in the other. So while we are complaining of heat in our *Summer*, people in the temperate lands on the other side of the Equator are shivering with the cold of their *Winter*, and when their turn comes for Summer it is winter here.

ARCTIC SCENE.

All the changes of the Seasons are brought about by the way in which the Earth moves round the Sun.

12. You see, therefore, that the *yearly* motion of the Earth causes the Seasons, and you know already that its *daily* motion gives us the changes of day and night.

LESSON XIII.

1. About Maps and the Compass.—In order to give us correct notions of the shape and size of countries, of the directions in which rivers flow, of the position of mountains, lakes, bays, islands, towns, and so on, we make a kind of picture that we call a *Map.*

A Map is a drawing of the Earth's surface or of some part of it.

2. Maps are hardly *pictures*, for they are not meant to show us different places as they would really appear to us, but only to give an idea of their position and size. On the next page there is a Map for you to look at.

On this Map the courses of rivers are marked by curved lines, mountains by thin wavy lines placed close together, towns by black dots. And if you turn to the Maps in a geographical Atlas, you will see that the countries are not only divided by little dotted lines, but are also painted in different colours.

3. The size of the Map has really nothing to do with the size of the country

nights short with us ?—When are they long ?—How many sets of temperate lands are there ?— Show me them on the globe.—*Explain, with the help of a globe and a lamp, how, on account of the inclination of the earth's axis to the plane of its orbit, the northern and southern hemispheres are more exposed to the rays of the sun at one time of the year than at another ; and how in consequence, when it is summer in England, it is winter in Australia, and vice versa.*

LESSON XIII.—What is a Map ?—Of what use is it ?—*Show the children how a person in a balloon, or a bird high in the air, would see a portion of the earth lying below like a map.*— What marks do we use on maps for rivers, mountains, towns ?—Find some of each.—Does a

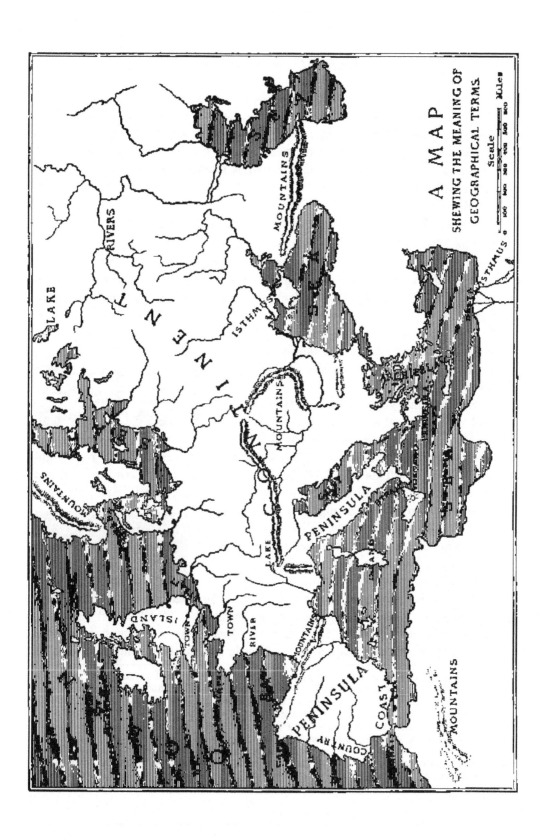

A MAP
SHEWING THE MEANING OF
GEOGRAPHICAL TERMS

Scale
0   100   200   300   400   500   Miles

drawn on it, for the very same place may be drawn of any size we please. But at the corner or bottom of all good Maps you will observe a line divided into equal portions, each of which counts for a certain number of miles. This is the *Scale,* and by means of it we can measure any distance on the Map. For instance, if the scale marks fifty miles for what is only drawn as *one inch,* then any five inches on the drawing show you a distance of 250 miles, ten inches 500 miles, and so on.

The Scale of a Map enables us to measure distances on it.

4. The Map which is here shown you points out the forms of those various divisions of land and water that you have already learned. The water on it is shaded, but the white part represents the land. Look carefully at the words printed on this Map, and try to find other parts of the Map like those which they mark.

5. You can hardly understand the following lessons without learning the meaning of North South, East, and West, or (as they are called) the *Points of the Compass.*

POINTS OF THE COMPASS.

6. Stretch out your arms and turn towards the part of the sky where the Sun rises. We call it the East. You have behind you the West, where the Sun sets, your left arm is pointing to the North, and your right arm to the South. This is all very simple, and if you only see the Sun, you can at once tell in what direction you are going—North, South, East, or West.

But you might do so even at night (if the stars were shining), for there is one star, called the Pole Star, which is always in the northern part of the sky, and when once you know the North the other points are easily found out.

THE PLOUGH AND POLE STAR.

7. Sailors in old times made use of the Sun by day and the Pole Star by night to guide them in their voyages, but now they have a far better and surer plan. A piece of magnetised steel, called the magnetic needle, is balanced on a small

map really show the *size* of the country it represents?—What do I mean by a "scale"?—Find me the scale on the map before you.—If a scale is divided into *inches,* and each inch represents 100 miles, how many inches on the map measure 200 miles?—Look at the scale of this outline-map of Europe. Now see if you can tell me how far it is from the north of Great Britain to the south—how far across Italy, &c.—*Explain this question of the scale very clearly, and take examples from other maps.* —Of what use, then, is the scale?— With the help of this outline-map, find some peninsulas—mountains—islands—capes— bays—straits—an archipelago—three seas—a continent—a gulf—a lake—a channel—an ocean.—What are the "points of the compass"?—*Let the teacher go over the subject-matter of Pars. 6 and 8 in the way described in the lesson, first of all showing the children the north side* peg placed in the centre of a box, so that it can swing round freely in any direction. Now this needle has the strange power of always pointing towards the North, no matter which way the vessel may be going. By looking at the needle, the mariner can tell at all times, by day or by night, where the North is, where the South, the East, and the West, and steer his ship accordingly. Hence this most useful invention is known as the *Mariner's Compass.* Every ship carries one or more compasses.

8. Attached to the magnetic needle is a circular card, on which the points of the compass are marked. The direction between North and East is called *North-East ;* that between North and West, *North-West ;* that between South and West, *South-West ;* and that between South and East, *South-East.* The points of the compass are commonly indicated by the letters N., N.E., E., S.E., S., S.W., W., and N.W.

9. On all maps the North is at the top, so of course the South is to be found at the bottom, the East on the right hand side, the West on the left hand. The *Equator* runs towards East and West, the *Axis* from North to South.

LESSON XIV.

1. About Lines drawn on Maps.—You will see lines upon a map, some of them drawn *across* it, and others running from the top to the bottom.

PARALLELS AND MERIDIANS.

Now none of these lines are really found on the World itself, but they are drawn on our maps to show us the exact position of every place, and to help us when we want to learn how far one place may be from another.

2. You know what the Equator is. Well, all those lines that go from West to East, just like it, are named *parallels.* They are supposed to be exactly the same number of miles apart from each other, and by making use of them we can easily find the distance of any point to the north or south of

of the schoolroom.—Find what part of this room is north-west, east, south-west, north-east.—On the map show me north, south-east, south.—How does the Equator run on a map ?—In what way can you find the points of the compass at night ?—Of what use is the mariner's compass ?—Describe it.—*Explain "magnetic," referring to a common magnet or compass.*

LESSON XIV.—*Explain the meaning of the word* PARALLEL.—Do the lines drawn on maps really exist on the Earth ?—Why do we draw them on our maps ?—What are parallels ?—Show some.—Which are the longest parallels ?—[*Those nearest the Equator. Explain.*]—Does the distance between these parallel lines vary ?—Of what use are the parallels ?—Why

the Equator. These lines look curved on a flat map, but on a globe they are seen to be quite straight, running round the Earth in the same way as the Equator does.

The Latitude of a place is its distance north or south of the Equator.

The Parallels of Latitude are always the same distance apart. They are drawn north and south of the Equator, and run in the same direction as it does.

3. A second set of lines is drawn from the top to the bottom (that is, from north to south) of your maps. These lines all meet at the poles, and as the Earth is thickest at the Equator, they are farther away from each other when they cross it than they are elsewhere. The use of these lines, called *meridians,* is to show us the distance of any place to the east or west of some other place. There is a town named Greenwich, near to the great city of London, and the meridian which passes through it is called the *Meridian of Greenwich,* or the *first meridian.* You will always find *that* meridian marked O on your maps, and from it distances to the east and west are measured.

The Longitude of a place is its distance east or west of the Meridian of Greenwich.

The Meridians of Longitude are drawn from north to south on the maps, and are widest apart when they cross the Equator.

4. In addition to the Parallels of Latitude and Meridians of Longitude, there are other lines sometimes drawn on maps which you will require to know of.

A circle supposed to be placed near the North Pole is the *Arctic Circle.* Another circle, at the same distance from the South Pole, is the *Antarctic Circle.*

5. Two more circles, placed as far from the Equator as the Arctic and Antarctic Circles are from the Poles, are called the *Tropics.* The Tropic in the Northern Hemisphere has been named by astronomers the *Tropic of Cancer;* that in the Southern Hemisphere, the *Tropic of Capricorn.*

do all the parallels, except the Equator, look *curved* on a map?—*Show them on the globe.*— What do you mean by the latitude of a place?—*Show London.*—Is this city in north or south latitude?—*Point out some places in south latitude.*—What do you call the lines drawn from the top of the map to the bottom?—Where do these lines meet on the globe?—*Show on the globe why the meridians are not equally distant from each other throughout their whole length.*—Of what use are the meridians?—*Show the position of Greenwich and the course of its meridian.*—*Notice also several of the parallels and meridians on the various maps.*—Where are the meridians farthest apart?—What is the Arctic Circle?—The Antarctic Circle?— *Point them out on the globe, and also the two Tropics.*—Now name in succession all the circles met with on our map of the World, from the North Pole to the South Pole.

LESSON XV.—(Parts I. and II.)

(PART I.)—**1. About the Zones.**—The lines that we heard about at the end of the last chapter divide the Earth into five great bands, of which the widest is the one between the Tropics.

2. Now just remember what you were lately told about warm, cold, and temperate countries. You know that near the Equator are hot lands, near the Poles cold ones, and that the temperate parts of the World lie between them. Well, the five wide bands which the Polar Circles and the Tropics mark out upon our maps simply show us these parts of the earth more clearly.

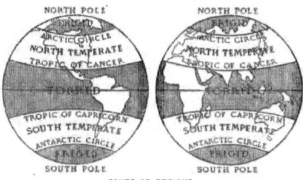

ZONES OR REGIONS.

3. The bands are called *zones* or *regions*. There are two Frigid (or Polar) Zones, two Temperate Zones, and one Torrid Zone—five altogether. Look at the little map and you will readily see where these zones are.

4. You see the broad belt or band on the picture, with the Equator passing straight across it. It is known as the *Torrid Zone*.

The lands that lie in the Torrid Zone are the warmest in the World. At some time of the year the Sun is exactly overhead there, and its beams are so hot that all work out-of-doors must be stopped. Nowhere else have we such numbers of plants, with beautiful, bright-coloured flowers, and the damp woods grow so thick that it is hardly possible to pass through them. The birds and butterflies of this Torrid Zone are as gaily coloured as its flowers; but great numbers of fierce wild animals, of poisonous snakes and troublesome insects, make the countries that lie between the Tropics much less delightful than they would otherwise be.

TROPICAL VEGETATION.

LESSON XV.—(PART I.)—Into how many different bands do the Tropics, Arctic and Antarctic Circles divide the Earth ?—Which is the widest of these bands ?—What do we call them ?—Two of these zones have cold countries ; name and show me them.—One contains the warmest parts of the world.—In what zones is the weather never very hot nor very cold ? —In which zone do we live ?—Tell me what you have learned about the heat of the Torrid

5. At the top and bottom of the little map you notice two more zones, the *North and South Frigid Zones*, which are marked off by the Arctic and Antarctic Circles. As the poles are in them, these regions are of course exceedingly cold, and indeed the land is covered with snow and the sea blocked up with ice for a great part of the year, or even the whole of it. Very few people care to live in such miserable countries, and the air is so chilly that there are no trees, and hardly any plants grow. But a good many large wild animals are found there, and the birds become wonderfully numerous, though they are never brightly coloured. In the long winter, most of the birds change their grey and brown tints for pure white. In these polar regions the Sun shines only for a portion of the year.

(PART II.)—6. The *Temperate Zones* are the parts between the Torrid and Frigid Zones. You have heard a good deal about temperate countries already in the lesson on the Seasons, and you no doubt remember that the air is never too hot or too cold there, and that the weather changes continually, giving us Spring, Summer, Autumn, and Winter. In the Temperate Zones, too, the Sun is never quite overhead, and the length of the days and nights changes with the Seasons. There are great numbers of beautiful trees and plants in these zones,

but they do not grow in such thick masses nor with such gay flowers as those in the lands between the Tropics. The birds have not such bright feathers, though far more of them are good singers than in the Torrid Zone. Then, again, fierce wild animals are not at all common, but there are plenty of animals useful to mankind, such as the horse, cow, and sheep.

TEMPERATE VEGETATION.

7. If you will look carefully again at the map which shows you all these zones or regions, you will observe that a very large part of the land on the

Zone—its flowers and plants—its animals.—What dangers and annoyances have people to endure who live in such hot countries !—*You might name some particulars about the chief wild animals of the Tropics, such as the tiger, lion, elephant, and camel ; and plants, such as maize, rice, sugar-cane, and cotton.—The almost impenetrable growth and the gloom of tropical forests should be mentioned.*—Tell me the most striking points you have learned about the Frigid Zones—their snow and ice, plants, birds, long winter.—*Short notice of the polar bear, reindeer, Esquimaux, Arctic expeditions.*

(PART II.)—What kind of weather makes a country *temperate ?*—Where are the Temperate Zones ?—Name the Seasons of temperate countries, and tell me something about each of them.—What do you know about the trees and plants of the Temperate Zones, the birds, wild animals, useful animals.—*Short account of such temperate productions as our common*

Earth lies in the North Temperate Zone, and that there is very little land in the South. In the countries of the Temperate Zones are found the most active and learned people in the world. We should try to know as much as possible about the Temperate Zones, for it is in the North one that we ourselves live.

8. Now I hope you will bear in mind all that has been said here about parallels, meridians, and other lines drawn on maps, and that you will not be so foolish as to fancy that they *really* exist on the surface of the Earth itself. We only put them on our maps to help us in learning many useful things about the Earth, and some of those things I have now told you.

There are five Zones—the Torrid, North and South Temperate, North and South Frigid. They are marked out by the Tropics of Cancer and Capricorn, and by the Arctic and Antarctic Circles.

LESSON XVI.

1. About Climate.--You will often hear the word *climate*, so I must tell you what it means.

The climate of a country is simply the kind of weather usually found in it, whether wet or dry, cold or hot.

Thus if a great deal of rain falls in any land we say it has a *wet* climate, or if the sun always shines so powerfully on it that the air is very hot, even in winter, we call its climate *warm.*

2. Hot climates are, of course, most commonly found in the countries which lie in the Torrid Zone, mild and cool climates in the Temperate Zones, and very cold climates in the Arctic and Antarctic Zones. But there are, besides, some other things which help to make differences in climate.

3. *The higher a place the colder it is.* Valleys are always warmer than hill tops, and some of the high mountains in the Torrid Zone have almost *all* kinds of climate on their sides. At the bottom the air is extremely warm,

fruits and grains, timber trees, &c.—Look at the map and tell me which of the zones has most land in it—which least land.—In what zone do we live ?—What have you been told respecting the people of this zone ?—Do the circles of which we have been talking *really* exist on the globe ?—Once more say how many zones there are.—Name the circles dividing them.

LESSON XVI.—What is climate ?—If much rain fell in any land what would you call its climate ?—If the Sun always shone very powerfully on some other country its climate would be ——?—In what parts of the Earth do most hot countries lie ?—Cold countries ?—Temperate countries ?—Are high places colder or hotter than low ones ?—What varieties of climate would you expect to find on a mountain within the tropics ?—Are any parts of the

higher up it becomes cooler and more temperate, while at the very top the snow lies on the ground all through the year. Indeed, a traveller climbing a high mountain within the tropics would have as many changes of weather as if he were going from the Equator to the North or South Pole. And there are many table-lands, or high plains, in the Torrid Zone quite as cold as the low lands in the temperate regions of the Earth, simply because they are raised up to a great height.

4. Places near the sea have generally mild weather throughout the whole year, for the soft breezes blowing from the water prevent too great heat in summer or too great cold in winter. Moreover, the sea, which has itself almost always the same amount of heat, makes the countries bordering upon it cooler in the summer months, warmer in the winter months.

5. Places, however, which are far distant from the ocean have a warm climate in summer and a very cold one in winter. So you see that the people who live in islands do not know anything of the great changes of weather that come upon those who dwell in the middle of a large continent, for, as I have said, the sea either cools the air or warms it, according to the season of the year.

6. In the British Islands (where you have always lived) the winds blow very often from the south-west, and bring us warm, rainy weather; but when the east winds come (as they mostly do) in early spring, the air becomes bitterly cold and dry.

7. The climate is always more or less wet if many trees grow in a country, and if there are very few trees it is sure to be dry. In some lands rain never falls at all, and then they become wretched *deserts*. We have learned something about these deserts already in the lesson on *Rain*. (See page 19.)

The nearer a country is to the Pole, the colder is its climate ; but the nearer to the Equator, the warmer.

High lands are colder than low ones.

Islands and places near the sea have mild climates' all the year round, but in the middle of the continents the summers are much warmer and the winters colder.

Many trees make a climate wet.

Torrid Zone cold ?—Why ?—In what way does the sea affect climate ?—*Compare the climate of a country lying far inland (such as Germany) with one surrounded by the sea (such as Great Britain.)*—Which people have the greatest changes of weather, those inland or those by the sea ?—What winds bring heat and wet to England ?—What effect has the east wind here ?—*Show the reasons.*—What effect have trees on a climate ?—*Give as examples the great damp of Western Canada, the drought of Spain, &c.*—For much interesting information on this subject see "Ansted's Physical Geography," pp. 451-460.

LESSON XVII.—(Parts I. and II.)

(PART I.)—**1. About the Plants and Animals of the World.**—We have already learned something about the plants and animals of the five zones, and have seen how they differ according to the amount of heat or cold in the air. I told you of the rich abundance of the trees and herbs of the tropics, the splendour of the birds' bright feathers, the enormous variety of insects. You heard, also, how numerous in these warm lands are snakes and fierce wild animals.

2. Again, I have spoken of the bleak, cold lands near the Poles, where men

REINDEER AND POLAR BEAR.

are few, but birds are many, and there are a considerable number of wild animals, such as the reindeer and the polar bear. In these remote parts the intense cold of the long winter is not overcome by the extremely short summer, so that plants have not the chance of growing to any size; while in many places the ground never loses its mantle of snow, and not even a blade of grass can live.

3. Then you will remember even better the description I gave you of your own temperate lands, blessed with the changing seasons and no extremes of

EUROPEAN ANIMALS—OTTER, CHAMOIS, RED DEER.

heat or cold. You should be well acquainted with the plants and animals you see every day around you; the useful timber trees, the sweet fruits, the pretty flowers, the tuneful birds, and the common domestic animals. All these abound in temperate climates.

4. So you see the different zones have different sorts of living creatures, both plants and animals, and the following sentence is, therefore, at once true and easily understood :—

Each climate has its own kinds of plants and animals.

LESSON XVII.—(PART I.)—What have we learned already [Lesson XV.] about the growth of plants in the Torrid Zone ?—About the birds, insects, snakes, wild animals ?—Do birds abound near the poles ?—What can you say of their colours ?—Do you know who the Esquimaux are ?—What plants are plentiful near the poles ?—*Explain how the description applies mainly to the Arctic regions, and how we know but little of the Antarctic.*—Tell me something about the plants of temperate climates—the names of some of the wild animals,

5. You know that the climate of a country depends, to a great extent, upon its *height above the sea*, so that if you could contrive to climb up a lofty mountain in the tropics you would pass through Torrid, Temperate, and Arctic Zones, reaching at last the never-melting snow of its summit. It would not, therefore, surprise you, during your ascent, to meet with different sorts of plants, and different animals, too, as you gradually got out of the hot air into the cooler air above. It would be like taking a journey from the Equator to the North Pole on the plains below.

AMERICAN ANIMALS—BISON, GRIZZLY BEAR, MONKEY, MUSK-OX, PECCARY.

6. Now there is another very important thing which I want you to look into and learn carefully. *Not only* do the plants and animals differ in the zones according to climate, but you will find that the different lands *in the same zone* have different sorts. Understand me clearly. Look at your Map of the World, and name for me the great divisions of the land lying partly in the North Temperate Zone.

There are three—North America, Europe, Asia. Well, the North American plants are not like those of Asia, and the plants of Europe are different from either. The animals are unlike also. Yet the Temperate Zone stretches over all three. Take another example: the centre of Africa and the northern part of South America are both crossed by the Equator, and

AFRICAN ANIMALS—ELEPHANT, HIPPOPOTAMUS, RHINOCEROS, LEOPARD, CAMELOPARD.

have the same amount of burning heat from the Sun. Yet neither the plants nor the animals of South America are the least like those of Africa.

domestic animals, singing birds.—*Explain "tropics."*—If I were to climb a mountain in the tropics (*i.e.*, Torrid Zone), through what zones should I pass?—Should I see the same kinds of plants all throughout my ascent?—Have all lands in a single zone the same animals and plants?—Name three great continents in the North Temperate Zone which have different natural productions.—*Give as examples if you like (that is, if you have pupils more than usually intelligent), turkey and opossum, magnolia* (America), *nightingale and chamois, myrtle* (Europe), *tiger and golden pheasant, tea* (Asia).—What two continents crossed by the Equator have very different animals? *Examples: boa and puma* (America), *hippopotamus and giraffe* (Africa). *If you have pictures of these you might show them, but do not burden the children's memories unnecessarily with new names.*

(PART II.)—7. Every country to which we may travel has some peculiar kinds of animals not found elsewhere, and plants which grow nowhere else. The farther we go, the greater becomes the difference. If we were to start from

ASIATIC ANIMALS—CROCODILE, TIGER, ANTELOPE, PYTHON, OX.

England, for instance, and pass through warmer countries, then through the still hotter regions of the Tropics, cross the Equator, reach cool lands again, and find ourselves in one of the few countries of the South Temperate Zone, we should now seek in vain for the plants and animals of our native land. Indeed, upon close observation, we should at length discover that every part of the South Temperate Zone was wholly unlike the North Temperate Zone in its living creatures, though the climates of the two zones were almost the same.

Even when the climates of two distant countries are the same, their plants and animals greatly differ.

8. Such is the natural arrangement of life on our globe. Variety is everywhere. Climate makes part of this variety, but no close resemblance of climate can make two far distant lands have the same beasts and birds, the same trees and flowers. God has made innumerable kinds of living beings to people His earth.

DOMESTIC ANIMALS—HORSE, SHEEP, ETC.

9. Man is the most intelligent and most powerful of all created beings. He has found means to tame many wild animals, and to take the best of the fruits of the earth for his own use. Wherever man has settled he has always carried with him the various *domestic* animals—that is to say, the animals used in and about his home. Among such are the horse, cow, sheep, and dog, and these (though flourishing best in a temperate climate)

(PART II.)—If we were to take a long voyage to a land in the Southern Temperate Zone, should we find the plants and animals of our Temperate Zone ?—Name from the map some southern temperate lands.—What causes this immense variety of kinds ?—How do you know that it is not climate only which makes the variety ?—What animals has man taken

are now found in nearly every part of the world that man himself can inhabit.

10. Many kinds of useful grains and fruits have also been brought from one country to another by man; and so there is now hardly a temperate land where wheat or barley or rye is not sown to give us flour for our daily bread. In warm countries rice, and *maize* (called Indian Corn), are largely grown for the same purpose. We have in England great numbers of flowers and fruits, of birds and four-footed animals, which were not here in old times, but are natives of countries which, though distant from England, have a climate the same as our own. These animals and plants have been brought here for our use or our pleasure, and in the same way the living productions of any climate may be removed by man to another climate like it, and will often flourish there as well as they did in their own country.

FARMYARD—COW, PIGS, ETC.

Domestic animals are found wherever man is found.

The plants and animals of any part of the world will usually live when removed to another part, if they continue to have the same climate.

LESSON XVIII.—(Parts I. and II.)

(PART I.)—**1. About the Races of Man.**—As there are differences in the plants and animals of the various parts of the Earth, so are there differences in mankind.

2. These differences, however, are most likely caused only by climate and manner of life, for we believe that all men have sprung from one family. But since they are now divided into at least five distinct sets, we may look upon each set as a separate *race*.

3. The five races are these—*white* men, *black* men, *red* men, *yellow* men,

with him from their native homes into all parts of the world?—What name is given to animals thus used by man?—What grains does man grow in temperate climates?—In warm climates? *Give, as examples of introduced plants and animals, the peacock and grey rat, American river-weed and potato, into England; the horse into South America, sheep into Australia. This is a very interesting subject to children, and one which can be well illustrated by a skilled teacher.*

LESSON XVIII.—(PART I.)—Are the men of one part of the world just the same as in all other parts?—What makes the difference between them?—How many varieties of men are there?—What name would you give to these varieties?—Name the five races.—To

and *brown* men. But it is not in colour only that they are unlike, for their ways of living and their customs and habits are very different.

4. White men form by far the most important race, for they have the best laws, the greatest amount of learning, and the most excellent knowledge of farming and trade.

FIVE GREAT TYPES OF MANKIND.

White.	Yellow.	Red.	Brown.	Black.
(*English.*)	(*Chinese.*)	(*American Indian.*)	(*South Sea Islands.*)	(*Negro.*)

There are five great races of men, and of these the white race is the highest.

5. Many tribes of men are almost constantly at war with each other, and

SAVAGES.

hardly know how to build houses, to till the ground, or to make any useful articles. They live merely on the fruits of the earth or the animals they kill, and they are so ignorant and unlearned that they are only a little superior to wild animals. These people are called *savages.*

6. But there are other tribes far superior to them in learning and know-

which race do we belong?—Is our race the highest?—What are savages?—What do I mean by *civilised* people?—If a race is half savage, what is it called?

Show the children (1) *how savages till the soil very rudely or not at all, subsist by hunting and fishing, do not know the use of metals, have no written language. Tell them, again,* (2) *of barbarous races, with abundant herds and flocks, generally living in tents and moving about, depending little on the cultivation of the soil. And let them see the degraded state of the women in both cases, the constant plunder and warfare, the total disregard of human life, the want, or debased forms, of religion. Give as examples* (1) *the American Indians, negroes of Africa, and aborigines of Australia;* (2) *the wandering tribes of Tartary and the Arabs.*

Next proceed to half-civilised races, who build houses and vessels, raise crops from the land, have some degree of learning, can manufacture many goods (though seldom with taste or great skill), but do not advance with the times, being suspicious of strangers and disliking commerce. Mention as examples the Chinese and Turks. Show how the Japanese are fast progressing out of this state.

ledge, who live in houses and towns, are skilled in matters concerning trade and farming, and are able both to make every article that they require and to obtain useful things from every part of the world. These are *civilised* people.

CIVILISED PEOPLE.

7. White men are nearly all civilised, and many of the yellow race are not far behind them. Some among the other three races of men have civilisation also, but by far the most of them are savages, or in that half-savage state we call *barbarous.*

(PART II.)—1. **About Men's Occupations.**—In order that they may be able to have food, clothing, and shelter, all men have to employ themselves in different ways. Savages do little more than hunt and fish; but people

AGRICULTURE.

who have some amount of civilisation are also engaged in *agriculture, grazing, manufacture,* and *commerce.*

Lastly, tell of the high degree of civilisation attained by the nations of Europe and North America ; the excellence of their manufactures ; their skilful agriculture ; their abundance of books ; their painting and sculpture ; their commerce with every part of the world that can afford them articles of use or luxury, or can buy their goods ; their colleges and schools ; their hospitals and charities ; their knowledge of the heavenly bodies ; their worship of the true God.

The distribution of the races of man should be pointed out on the map in this way :—

I.—*White (civilised), dwelling especially in Europe, but spreading through America and every part of the world.*

II.—*Black (savage) in Africa. Large numbers, half-civilised, in America, originally brought from Africa as slaves.*

III.—*Yellow (half-civilised or barbarous) in Asia, Turkey, Japan, Lapland and Finland, Arctic regions.*

IV.—*Brown (barbarous or savage) in Pacific Islands, Australia, and Malay Peninsula.*

V.—*Red (barbarous or savage). The original inhabitants of North and South America.*

The rapid decay of the two last races since the introduction of white men might be noticed.

(PART II.)—*Why is it necessary for man to work ?—What work is done by savages ?—*

2. Those who till the land and make it produce crops of wheat and other grains, potatoes, fruits, and so on, are said to be employed in *agriculture*, and are called farmers.

3. Some persons have large flocks of sheep and herds of oxen, which they feed on grassy fields for the sake of their milk and their flesh. The sheep's

SHEPHERD AND SHEEP.

wool, too, can be made into warm cloth, and the cow's hide is formed into leather by tanning, so that these animals are very profitable to their owners. Farmers nearly always keep cattle and sheep, but in some parts of the world there are tribes of men who constantly move about from place to place, and own almost nothing but immense numbers of oxen, sheep, or horses. In our own land, too, many people keep farms simply for the feeding of oxen and sheep. They are called *graziers*.

4. All things *made* either by the hands or machinery are called *manufac-*

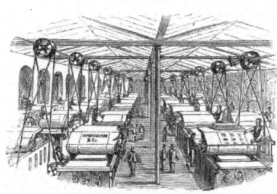

INTERIOR OF MANUFACTORY.

tures, such as cloth, paper, glass, tools, carts, and anything else that is not *found*, but has to be *made* by man for his use.

5. *Commerce* is the exchange of articles made or found in any land for the productions of some other country. Thus our merchants send ships abroad laden with cloth, iron goods, coals, and other things which they can supply, and they receive back goods that are required in England, such as grain, cotton, sugar, tea, wine, timber, and

Name some of the employments of civilised people.—Tell me some things done by farmers. —What other name is given to farming?—Name some crops the farmer raises in England. —*Show how farming is less necessary in hot countries owing to the abundance of wild vegetable productions.*—What are graziers?—Why can grazing be successfully managed in places where crops could not be grown?—*Details of sheep-grazing in the Highlands and Australia; cattle-grazing in Ireland.—Explain* " live stock."—Tell me what we obtain from the cow and the sheep.—Are herds always kept in the same fields?—What are manufactures?— Name some.—What kinds of manufactures are the most useful?—[*Those for food, dress, and shelter; give examples.*] Would you expect to find the manufacture of many articles amongst an uncivilised nation?—Why not?—What is commerce?—Tell me some goods sent out from England—other goods brought into England.—What are exports?—imports?

cattle. We call the articles sent *out* of a country its *exports*, and the goods brought back in return are the *imports*.

6. The employments of which we have been learning are the principal occupations of mankind, but there are many other. trades and professions. Everyone in the world both can be busy and should

QUAY-SIDE—SHIP LOADING.

be busy in some way. Even boys and girls at school are usefully employed when they learn their lessons carefully, and thus prepare their minds for the occupation which they must by-and-by undertake.

LESSON XIX.

1. About Government.—In every civilised country there must be rules, or laws, by which the people may be bound. No one can be allowed to injure his neighbour or rob him of his property without punishment. If there were no laws, and each person did merely what pleased him best, the country would soon come to ruin.

2. Savages have few rules or laws, because with them the strongest makes the weaker obey him through simple fear, and they have little property worth taking care of. Besides, from their ignorance of right and wrong, they do not think of telling people what they ought to do, and what they should avoid.

3. All civilised people see the importance of having good laws, and they either allow themselves to be governed by some person chosen as their ruler, or they make laws themselves.

4. An *Empire* is a form of government in which a person called

QUEEN READING SPEECH BEFORE PARLIAMENT.

—There are many other employments of mankind beside these. Name some. [*Useful examples of employments are these—fishing, sailing, mining, professions, fighting for one's country, shopkeeping.*]—What is the best employment for children?

LESSON XIX.—What is a law?—Why do people need laws?—What kind of countries have the best laws?—Why have savages few laws?—How does a civilised country get its laws?—*Tell the children how the laws are made in England.*—What is an Empire?—a

an *Emperor* is the head.   In a *Kingdom* the chief ruler is the *King* or *Queen*. Emperors have generally more power over their subjects than Kings.   Each of these governors is called a *Sovereign*, or *Monarch;* he holds his post for life, and his eldest son or nearest heir succeeds him.

5. In many Kingdoms the *Sovereign* has only a *limited* power, but in some other Kingdoms, and in most Empires, the Sovereign's own will regulates the country, and he has the most complete command over the lives and property of all his people.   He is what is called an *absolute* monarch.

6. When a nation appoints its own governors, and can change them at any time, the country is a *Republic*.   In this form of government everyone is considered equal.   A number of men are chosen from time to time to make the laws and manage the country's affairs.   They may select some one as head or *President*, but he only holds his power for a few years, and he may be succeeded by any person the people like to name.

LESSON XX.

1. **About Political Divisions.**—The word *political* looks hard, but I think I can readily make you understand it.   You have been learning till now much about the *natural* divisions of the world—that is to say, its divisions as they exist in nature.   But there are other divisions no less important, which man has to make for his own purposes, and these we call *political* divisions.

2. I might give as examples of natural divisions—capes, bays, islands, straits, seas, none of these being made by man, and all of them changeable by nature alone.   When I speak, however, of political divisions, I mean such things as kingdoms, empires, republics, cities, towns, and villages.   Men can change these as much as they please ; kingdoms may become larger or smaller, old towns may decay and at last disappear, new towns may be built.   So if you could look at a map only a hundred years old, and compare it with a new one, you would find many alterations in the countries, and many new towns, but you would find the mountains, rivers, and other natural divisions unaltered.

Kingdom ?—What name is given both to Emperors and Kings ?—When a King or Emperor dies, who succeeds him ?—Is a King's power always unbounded ?—If he has complete power over his people, what is he said to be ?—What is a Republic ?—*Give some account of the United States, its Congress and President.*—Does the President of a Republic hold his power for life ?—*Show how most of the governments of the New World are Republics, and of the Old World Kingdoms or Empires.*—*Explain* "absolute" *and* "*monarch.*"

Lesson XX.—What do we call such divisions of the world as seas, islands, peninsulas, and rivers ?—Can man change natural divisions ?—*Tell about the Suez Canal, made by man to connect two seas.   Then show how natural causes change natural features, as, for instance, in the deltas of the Nile and Mississippi, the inroads of the sea on the coast of Holland, and the formation of coral islands.   [See "Ansted's Physical Geography."]*—Are latitude and longitude connected with natural or political geography ?—Tell me some political divisions.

3. I will now tell you some important political divisions. A *state* is generally only another word for a whole *nation* or *country*, although in some

CITY—RIVER—SHIPPING (BELFAST).

parts of the world it means a very large division of a nation. *Provinces* are large divisions of countries, and *counties* smaller ones.

4. When a very large number of houses have been built close together we call them a *city*. A *town* is smaller than a city, and a *village* only contains a few houses. In England we are accustomed to give the name of city to any

LINCOLN CATHEDRAL.

town which has a cathedral. Many of these cathedral cities are little more than villages in size.

5. The *capital* of a country is the place in which the laws are made, and in which the Sovereign generally resides. It is very frequently (though not

—Notice, if you like, the destruction of old kingdoms (Assyria, the Roman Empire, Poland), old cities (Troy, Nineveh, Indian cities of America); add also an account of the rapid rise of some new countries (United States, Belgium, Italy), and new towns (New York, Birkenhead, Middlesboro').—What differences should we find between a very old map and a new one ?—What two things may the word "state" mean ?—What is a province ?—a county ?— a city ?—a town ?—a village ?—Is a city always a large place ?—Explain "cathedral."—

D

always) a large city. Each of those divisions of England known as counties has its own chief town, called either the *county town* or capital.

LESSON XXI.

1. About Religions.—*Religion means the worship of a God.* Most men have a belief of some kind in the existence of a Great Being to whom they owe respect, and there are few, no matter how savage they may be, who have no idea at all of a future life. But an immense number of people have never even heard of the true GOD who made all things, and have false gods alone to worship. They are called *Heathens* or *Pagans*.

HEATHEN IDOLS.

2. Some Pagans worship idols of their own making, others worship animals, and others make the heavenly bodies their gods. A better class of Heathens

MOSQUE OF ST. SOPHIA, CONSTANTINOPLE.

have some dim ideas of an unseen and almighty Creator, but they have not learned the truths of the Gospel.

3. The largest sect of Pagans is that of the *Buddhists*, who number at least one-fourth of the inhabitants of the globe. The *Brahmin* religion is another heathen form of worship with a great many believers.

4. The false religion known as *Mohammedan* was founded by Mohammed, a native of Arabia, who called him-

What is the capital of a country?—Tell me two names for the principal town of an English county.

LESSON XXI.—*Explain the term* RELIGION.—Are there many people without any form of religion ?—Have all people heard of the true God ?—What are Pagans ?—What do they worship ?—Are there any heathens of a better kind ?—Name two great sects of Pagans.— *Explain the word* SECT.—*Show the distribution of Buddhists (China) and Brahmins (India), as well as other kinds of heathens.*—Who are the Mohammedans ?—*Show where they are*

self the prophet of the true God. The *Jews* are a singular nation, long scattered about the world without any land of their own. They believe in the Old Testament, but not in the New, for they think that the Saviour has not yet come.

5. About a third of mankind are called *Christians*. They believe that JESUS CHRIST is the Saviour of the world, and that the Old and New Testaments contain God's Word. The Christian religion—the only true one—is spreading steadily over all the earth. The highest civilised nations are Christian, and they send *missionaries* to the most distant parts of the world to preach the Gospel to the Heathen, and to raise them from their ignorance and sin.

chiefly found [Turkey, Northern Africa, Western Asia].—Where do the Jews live?—What is their belief?—What do Christians believe?—How does their belief differ from that of the Jews?—Are there more Pagans than Christians? [*about half as many more.*]—*A few particulars of the distribution of the three great Christian divisions—Roman Catholic (Ireland, Southern Europe, South America), Greek Church (Russia and Greece), Protestant (England, North Europe, North America, British Colonies).*—Is the Christian religion spreading?— What are missionaries?—*Show some mission stations on the map.*

TABLES.*

THE EARTH'S CIRCUMFERENCE is	.	.	. 25,000 miles.
THE EARTH'S DIAMETER is	.	.	. 8,000 „

* The diameter at the equator is about 26 miles longer than the diameter at the poles (where the earth is slightly flattened).

THE SURFACE OF THE EARTH covers	.	200 millions of square miles.	
WATER . . .	„	. 148	„ „
LAND . . .	„	. 52	„ „
ASIA contains	.	. 17½ millions of square miles.	
AFRICA „	.	12	„ „
NORTH AMERICA „	.	8½	„ „
SOUTH AMERICA „	.	6½	„ „
OCEANIA „	.	4	„ „
EUROPE „	.	3½	„ „
THE EARTH'S INHABITANTS number	.	1,415 millions of human beings.	
ASIA has a population of	.	. 800	„ „
EUROPE . .	.	. 300	„ „
AFRICA . .	.	. 200	„ „
NORTH AMERICA .	.	. 60	„ „
OCEANIA .	.	. 30	„ „
SOUTH AMERICA .	.	. 25	„ „

* These Tables may be usefully committed to memory. The numbers contained in them are merely approximate *estimates* (especially those of population). They are put in the simplest form possible, as it is not desirable to load a young child's memory with lengthy strings of figures. An intelligent teacher will find the Tables of some value in giving an idea of the *relative* sizes and populations of the continents, a subject which a child cannot grasp without having learned something of their *actual* sizes and populations. In most elementary works on Geography, the number of inhabitants in the world is very much under-estimated.

LESSON XXII.

1. About the Hemispheres.—As the word *hemisphere* simply means *half a globe*, we might draw various pictures of hemispheres which would show us the Earth in a great number of different ways. But the halves of the World commonly represented on maps are the Eastern and Western, each of them showing a great land-mass, and each with the North Pole at the top, the South Pole at the bottom, and the Equator drawn across the middle.

2. Let us look at the maps of these two Hemispheres, and notice some things that are interesting in the great land-masses. In the Eastern Hemisphere lies the *Eastern Continent*, and in the Western Hemisphere lies the *Western Continent*. You can easily observe that the Western Continent is much smaller than the Eastern one.

3. Now glance for a moment at the two maps as they lie on the page before you. You see both sides of the World here at once, so try if you can make out the zone that has the most land in it. Also find whether most of the land is north or south of the Equator. And, lastly, observe the curious tongue or wedge-like shape of several of the large divisions of the land, broad at the north and pointed towards the south.

There is more land in the North Temperate Zone than in any other zone.

By far the greatest part of the land is on the north side of the Equator.

4. The **Eastern Continent,** or Old World, stretches broadly from east to west, very little of it coming south of the Equator. It has three great divisions (also sometimes called continents)—*Asia, Africa,* and *Europe.*

LESSON I.—What is a hemisphere ?—Name the hemispheres commonly drawn on maps. —What is at the top of the map ? at the bottom ? across the centre ?—If a map of the *Northern* and *Southern* Hemispheres were made, what would be the line surrounding them ?— What would be in the centre of each ?—What do you call the great land-mass in the Eastern Hemisphere ? in the Western ?—Which of these two continents is the larger ?—Which zone has most land in it ?—*Notice the little diagrams on the map of the hemispheres. Show from them that England is at the centre of the greatest extent of land, while New Zealand is in the middle of the greatest extent of water.*—Does most of the land lie north or south of the Equator ?—What is the shape of Africa ?—*Explain the word* WEDGE.—Find some more wedge-

5. *Asia*, the largest of the three divisions, is closely united to Europe. *Africa* comes next in size. It is a vast peninsula, joined on to Asia by the narrow isthmus of Suez. Africa is three times larger than Europe, Asia five times. But Europe, though the smallest, is still the most important great division of the World.

6. The **Western Continent** is long and rather narrow, stretching almost from pole to pole. It is made up of two great divisions, called North America and South America. These are very like one another, both in size and shape. They are joined by the isthmus of Panama. The two Americas together are not as large as Asia.

7. A small portion of Asia extends into the Western Hemisphere, and comes very close to North America, though it does not quite touch it.

8. The line formed by the sea-shore is called the *coast-line*, and when we compare the above-mentioned continents, or great divisions of land, with one another, we find that their coast-lines are longer or shorter in proportion to the size of the whole continent, according as their sea-shores are more or less regular in shape. For example, the sea-shores of Europe present so many "ins" and "outs," that its coast-line is actually *longer* than the whole coast-line of Africa, though (as you know) Africa is a far larger continent than Europe. Asia and North America have many bays, gulfs, peninsulas, and capes; hence they are said to have a *long* coast-line, while Africa and South America have so few large inlets and peninsulas that their coast-line is very *short*, when compared with that of the other continents.

9. The islands that lie close to the great divisions of land are said to belong to them. Asia and North America have a good many of these islands; Europe, Africa, and South America have only a few. Several very large islands lie near the North American coast.

10. The islands in the middle of the oceans, and that great island of Australia (which is nearly as big as Europe, and is itself sometimes called a continent), are placed in the sixth great division of the land, "Oceania."

11. *Oceania* extends through both the Eastern and Western Hemispheres.

---

like masses of land.—In which of the five zones is there most land?—How is the Eastern Continent divided?—Give another name for the Eastern Continent?—Which is the largest of the Old World continents? the next in size? the smallest? the most important?—*Show how Europe surpasses Asia and Africa in coast-line, fertility, climate, and civilisation.*—How is Africa united to Asia? Europe to Asia?—What separates Europe from Africa?—How far does the Western Continent extend?—Name its two parts?—What joins them?—What is their size taken together?—Which is the larger?—About how much larger is North America than Europe? [*more than twice.*]—Is there any part of the Old World continent in the Western Hemisphere? —What is the *coast-line?*—Is the African coast-line a long one for such a large continent?—Is the coast-line of Europe long? of South America? North America? Asia?—*Show the importance of coast-line as regards commerce and climate.*—Name some islands belonging to Asia.— [*Bear in mind that the so-called East Indian islands (Borneo, Java, &c.) are included by us in Oceania.* Some islands belong to Europe—to Africa—to North America—to South

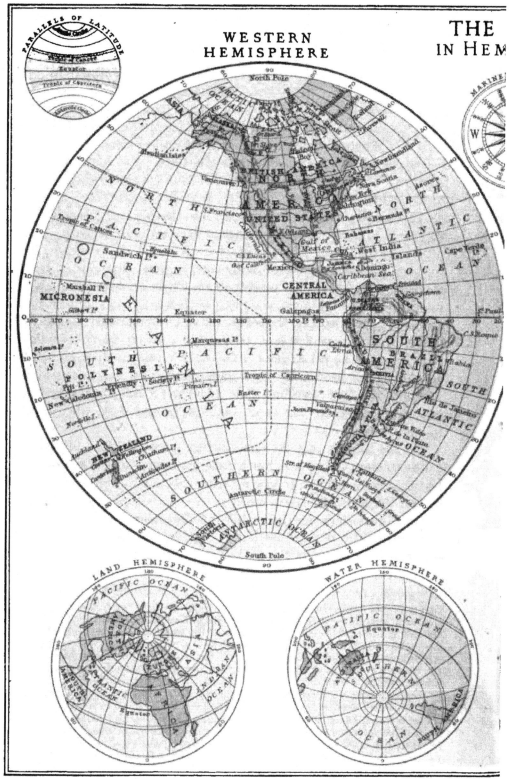

WESTERN
HEMISPHERE

THE
IN HEM

MARCUS WARD & CO., LONDON & BELFAST.

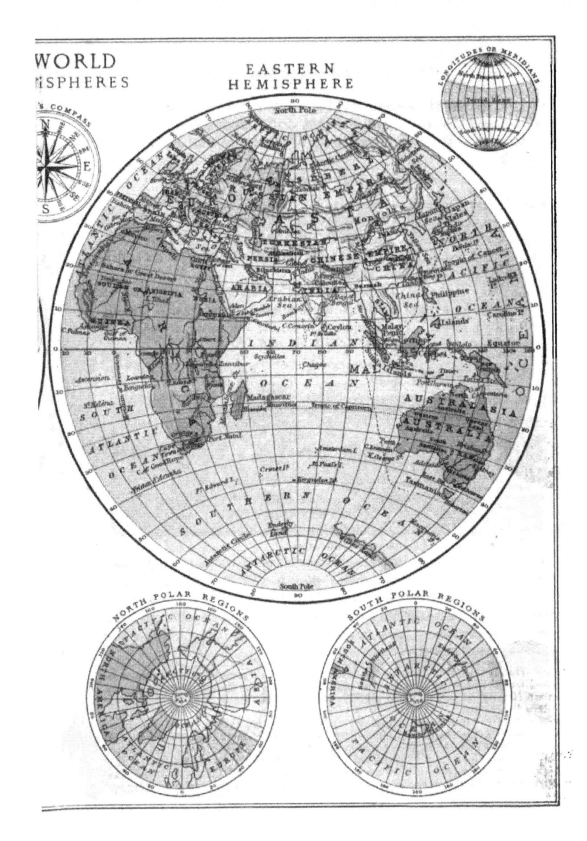

WORLD
MISPHERES

EASTERN
HEMISPHERE

There are six great divisions of the Earth—Asia, Africa, Europe, North and South America, and Oceania.   Of these Asia is largest, Europe smallest.   Oceania is made up of Australia and many scattered islands.

LESSON XXIII.

1. About the Oceans.—There are six oceans—the *Pacific, Atlantic, Indian, Southern, Arctic,* and *Antarctic Oceans.*   Now if you look carefully at your maps of the Hemispheres, you will find that these six oceans, thus distinguished by separate names, are in reality only portions of one great sea which surrounds all the dry land on this globe.

2. Among the numerous islands which you see scattered over the face of the Ocean, many have been built up by wonderful little animals, known as the *reef-making corals.*   The islands thus formed are called, according to their size and shape, *coral reefs, coral islands,* or *atolls.*

CORAL ISLAND OR ATOLL.

3. The *Pacific* Ocean is that great extent of water which separates Asia from America.   It covers about one-fourth of the surface of the earth.   The Pacific is almost shut in by land on the north, with only a small opening into the Arctic Ocean called Behring Strait; but it is very wide in its southern part, sometimes called the *South Sea.*   Several seas open into the Pacific on the west; but none on the east.

America.—What is Oceania ?—How far does it extend ?—Name a great island or continent in Oceania.—Name the principal islands of Oceania that are in the Eastern Hemisphere—in the Western Hemisphere and north of the Equator—those that lie south of the Equator in the Western Hemisphere.

LESSON XXIII.—How many oceans are there ?—What are they portions of ?—How are many islands in the Ocean built up?—*Give an account of the coral animal (wrongly called coral insect), and the reefs and atolls formed by it.*   [*See Somerville's, Page's, or Ansted's* "Physical Geography."]—How large is the Pacific ?—How is it bounded on the north ?—By what other name is the Southern Pacific known?—Name some of the seas which open into the Pacific on the west.—Are there any on the east side of this ocean ?—

4. The *Atlantic* Ocean is more than half the size of the Pacific. It stretches from north to south between the Old World in the east and the New World in the west. Many seas open into it from Europe and North America, but none from Africa and South America.

5. The *Indian* Ocean, much smaller than the Atlantic, divides Australia from Africa, and is only open on its southern side. It belongs for the most part to the Torrid Zone, and is subject to terrible storms, called *hurricanes*.

6. The *Southern* Ocean is the name applied to that wide expanse of water, with hardly any land in it, which is found to the south of the three Oceans just described, and fills up the space between them and the Antarctic Circle. In one part of it you might sail all round the world without touching land. *Icebergs*, very dangerous to ships, have been met with in every part of this ocean.

7. The *Arctic* Ocean is a smaller body of water, almost shut in by land, and with the North Pole nearly at its centre. Large *icefields* and *icebergs* block up the waters of this ocean, and until now have prevented navigators from reaching the North Pole.

8. Little is known about the *Antarctic* Ocean, a sea which surrounds the South Pole. Almost the whole space enclosed by the Antarctic Circle is covered with ice. It contains several large islands; one of these, named by its discoverer *Victoria Land*, is a country with very high mountains and volcanoes, and as large as Great Britain.

ICEBERGS IN THE ANTARCTIC.

What is the size of the Atlantic ?—What seas open into it from Europe—from North America ?—*Mention the " Sargasso Sea."*—Is the Indian Ocean large ?—How is it bounded on the north ?—Why is the Indian a warm ocean ?—*Explain the word* HURRICANE.—What are the limits of the Southern Ocean on the south—on the north ?—What is remarkable about this Ocean ?—How is the Arctic Ocean bounded ?—What lies at its centre ?—Is it easy to sail through the Arctic ?—*Describe an iceberg, and say something of the North-West Passage and of Arctic explorations.*—Is the Antarctic Ocean well known ?—Point out on the map some land in this ocean.—Would you expect to find inhabitants in the land near the South Pole ?

QUESTIONS ON THE MAP OF THE EASTERN HEMISPHERE.*

LESSON XXIV.

Continents, or Principal Divisions.—In what different ways is the word *continent* used?—What great divisions do you see in the map?
Name those that extend into the Western Hemisphere.
What immense island is in *Oceania*?—How is Asia joined to Africa?
Which great division has the most irregular coast?
What is an isthmus?
Which division is largest—Europe, Asia, or Africa?—Which is smallest?
Is Europe much larger than Australia?
In what great division are most of the islands?

Oceans.—*What is an ocean?*—Name all the oceans.
What oceans do you see on this map?—Which Polar Ocean has land round it?
What are the limits of the Southern Ocean?
What ocean lies between Africa and Australia?
Name the great division of land which lies north of the Indian Ocean.
What ocean is west of Africa and Europe?
What ocean is east of Asia and Australia?

Seas, Bays, and Gulfs.—*What is a sea? a gulf? a bay?*
Begin at the north and name all the seas on the east of Asia.
Are there many bays in Africa? many in Europe?
Tell me all the seas and bays you can find in Europe.—Which is largest?
What bays and seas are south of Asia?
What sea divides Africa from Europe?—Find all the seas which open into the Mediterranean.—Where is the Red Sea?
Tell me the names of some gulfs on the map.
Is there any real difference between gulf, bay, and sea?

Straits.—*What is a strait?*
Name the straits between the Mediterranean and the Atlantic—between England and the continent of Europe—between Australia and New Guinea—between Madagascar and Africa—between the Red Sea and the Indian Ocean.

Islands.—*What is an island?*—What great division is wholly made up of islands?—Is it in one hemisphere or in both?
Tell me the largest island on the map.—What is it sometimes called?
What islands are east of Asia—west of Europe—north of Europe—east of Africa—north of Australia—south of Asia?
What is the most western island of Europe?—What island is nearest the North Pole?—What islands lie in the Indian Ocean?
What are the chief islands of Oceania that lie in the Eastern Hemisphere?

LESSON XXV.

Rivers.—*What is a river?*
In what direction do most rivers flow in the far north of Europe and Asia?
What way do most of the rivers in Asia flow?
Are there many rivers in Australia? many in Africa?
What rivers do you see in Africa?—What rivers flow into the Indian Ocean?

* The map of the Hemispheres being on a small scale, it will be better to use a large wall map when practicable.

What African river enters the Mediterranean?
What river of Europe flows into the Black Sea—into the Caspian Sea?

Lakes.—*What is a lake?*
Is the Caspian a lake?—What lakes are in Africa?

General Questions.—Show me the Arctic and Antarctic circles—the Equator—the Tropics of Cancer and Capricorn—the North and South Poles?
Which set of lines is used for measuring latitude?
What do you call these lines?—Why are they called *parallels?*
Show me the meridians.—From what meridian do we measure longitude?—Find it.
What is a peninsula?
What way do most of the peninsulas point?—Name some of them.
What great division of land lies entirely to the north of the Equator—nearly to the north—partly south partly north—in both hemispheres?
Is there much land south of the Equator? much sea?
In what zone does the greater part of Europe lie?—Which zone has most land in it?
What zone is most of Africa in?—In what zones does Australia lie?
Name the tropic that crosses the north of Africa and south of Asia.
What is a cape?—Name some *capes* on the map.
Show me by what oceans you would sail from Europe to Australia.
How would you travel by land from the south of Africa to the west of Europe?
If you wanted to sail from the Black Sea to the British Islands, how would you go?
If you were sailing from Madagascar to Japan, through what seas would you pass?
Do we know much about the lands near the South Pole?—Why not?
*What do the numbers mean which are marked on the Equator?
*Where are the distances in latitude marked?

[* These two questions should be carefully explained by the teacher. The following facts ought also to be demonstrated by the help of a globe:— *Oceania lies in both hemispheres; the Eastern Hemisphere only contains a small part of the Atlantic and Pacific Oceans; a small part of Asia reaches into the Western Hemisphere; half of the Arctic Ocean is in each hemisphere, and half of the Antarctic and Southern Oceans also. England is at the central point of a hemisphere containing most of the land on the globe. New Zealand is the centre of a hemisphere containing most of the sea.*]

There are seven little drawings on the same sheet as the map of the Hemispheres. Two show the Parallels of Latitude and Meridians of Longitude, the Zones, &c. Two more display part of the Northern and Southern Hemispheres, showing the limits of the two Polar Oceans. The fifth is a hemisphere with the greatest amount of water; the sixth a hemisphere with the greatest amount of land. The seventh is a "Mariner's Compass."

QUESTIONS ON THE MAP OF THE WESTERN HEMISPHERE.

LESSON XXVL

Continents, or Principal Divisions.—*What is a continent?*—Has it any other meaning?—What great body of land lies entirely in the Western Hemisphere?
What names are given to its two divisions?
Which of them lies altogether to the north of the Equator?
How much of South America comes north of the Equator?
How are North and South America united?—*What is an isthmus?*
What separates North America from Asia? from Europe?
What great divisions of the land are *partly* seen in this hemisphere?

Islands.—*What is an island?*—Name the larger groups of islands which belong to Oceania.—*What is a large group of islands often called?*
　　Show me some islands on the east coast of America—on the north.
　　Are there many islands on the west coast of America?
　　Point out Greenland, the Azores, Bermudas, Cape Verdes, Falklands, Galapagos, Tierra del Fuego.—What is remarkable about the Aleutian Islands?

Capes.—*What is a cape?*—Show me Cape San Roque, Cape Farewell, Cape Lucas.
　　What cape comes at the south point of South America?—Is it on the mainland?

Straits.—*What is a strait?*—What is the most southerly strait in America?
　　What strait separates Greenland from the mainland?
　　What strait lies between Asia and North America?

Oceans.—What oceans are shown on this map?—Which seems to be the largest?
　　How does the Arctic Ocean open into the Pacific? into the Atlantic?
　　Which ocean has most islands?—To what great division of land do they belong?
　　Where is the Antarctic?—What land is in it?

Seas, Bays, and Gulfs.—*What is a sea—a bay—a gulf?*
　　Show me the Gulf of Mexico and the Caribbean Sea.—Would you expect their waters to be warm?—Why?
　　Are there any large bays in South America?
　　What bays are on the west coast of North America?
　　Show me Hudson's Bay.—Are its waters likely to be cold or hot?—Why?

LESSON XXVII.

Rivers.—*What is a river?*
　　Do many rivers flow into the Pacific from America? many into the Atlantic?
　　Why is this?—In what direction does the greater part of America slope?
　　Which ocean receives most river-water from America?
　　Show me three great rivers in South America.—In what direction do they flow?
　　Name one South American river north of the Equator.
　　Which river seems to be the largest in South America?
　　What very large river falls into the Gulf of Mexico?—Look at the map of North America, and tell me its largest branches, and point out where they rise.
　　Show a North American river which falls into the Arctic Ocean.

Lakes.—*What is a lake?*—Find a river in North America flowing through several lakes.—Show other lakes in North America.
　　Do you see any large lakes in South America?

General Questions.—Look at this map, and then at the map of the Eastern Hemisphere.—Tell me which has the most land in it.
　　Which is wider—the Old or New World?—Which is longer?
　　What is an isthmus?—Find one on the map.
　　What is a peninsula?—Show me a peninsula in America which points to the north.—Is this usual?—Find some more peninsulas.
　　Name some islands and the mouth of a river which are on the Equator.
　　What tropic crosses South America? North America?
　　Which is the only zone that contains no part of America?
　　Through what seas and oceans would you pass if you were to sail from the mouth of the River Mississippi to Behring's Straits? from Ceylon to Vancouver's Island?
　　How does Europe lie with regard to South America? New Zealand?
　　In what direction from North America are the West Indian Islands—Africa—the Galapagos Islands—Behring's Straits—Australia—the Cape Verde Islands?

CPSIA information can be obtained
at www.ICGtesting.com
Printed in the USA
BVOW09s1049011216

469419BV00010B/94/P

9 781287 915980